STEP-BY-STEP
MAKING JEWELLERY

SARA GRISEWOOD
ILLUSTRATED BY JIM ROBINS

KINGfISHER

KINGFISHER
Kingfisher Publications Plc
New Penderel House
283–288 High Holborn
London WC1V 7HZ

First published by Kingfisher Publications
Plc 1995
This edition published 2000

10 9 8 7 6 5 4 3 2 1
1TR/1199/SC/(HBM)/128JMA

A CIP catalogue record for this book
is available from the British Library.

ISBN 1 85697 325 5

Series editor: Deri Robins
Editor: Clare Oliver
Series designer: Ben White
Illustrator: Jim Robins
Photographer: Steve Shott
Cover designer: Terry Woodley

Printed in Hong Kong/China

CONTENTS

WHAT YOU NEED

You don't need expensive equipment or materials to make jewellery. You can use shells, felt and leaves, as well as home-made papier mâché and salt dough. Read all the instructions before you start, to make sure that you have everything you need.

Paint

Varnish

Flour

Special Things

Findings are the special fastenings used to make jewellery. Necklaces can be tied with a knot, but you'll need findings for badges and earrings.

Craft shops sell findings, as well as beads, sequins and fake gemstones.

Paper-clips are ideal for pendant hooks – just stick them into the jewellery before baking. For threading heavy beads, buy a strong thread, such as linen carpet thread.

Wallpaper paste

Rolling pin

Coloured clay

Salt

SAFETY TIP
Craft knives, needles and skewers are very sharp. Ask an adult to help when you use them.

Tools of the Trade

You'll need scissors, a craft knife, glue (a safe but strong epoxy glue), a pencil, metal ruler, masking tape, sewing thread and needles.

An ordinary knife, fork and spoon and a rolling pin make ideal tools for modelling. Work on an old board. Bake beads on kebab skewers.

Buy ready-coloured clay such as Fimo™. Keep paper and wall-paper paste to hand for papier mâché, and flour, salt and water for salt dough (see page 6). You'll also need paints, brushes and varnish (see pages 8–9).

String

Needle

Felt

Shell

Strong thread

Skewer

Brush

Newspaper

Craft knife

Modelling tools

Findings

Epoxy glue

Scissors

Bought beads

Leaves

5

BASIC TECHNIQUES

Ready-coloured clay is ideal for making jewellery, and doesn't even need a coat of paint. Other modelling materials, such as salt dough and papier mâché can be made at home very cheaply.

Making Salt Dough

Stir together 100 grams of salt with 340 grams of sieved plain flour. Slowly add 225-350 ml of lukewarm water.

Mix together to make a soft dough. Knead until smooth, then leave it in a plastic bag for half an hour before using.

Bake your pieces at Gas Mark 2, 170°C. Beads and badges will take about $\frac{1}{2}$-$1\frac{1}{2}$ hours. Ask an adult to tap them, and if they sound hollow, they are ready.

Most wallpaper pastes contain fungicide, which is poisonous. Always buy a non-fungicide paste, and be careful to follow the instructions on the packet.

Making Papier Mâché

Old cereal boxes will make ideal card bases for your jewellery. Cover your base with layers of torn newspaper dipped in wallpaper paste. The smaller the strips, the smoother your jewellery will be. Let the papier mâché dry between layers.

Using Coloured Clay

You can buy coloured clay from craft shops and toy shops – it even comes in metallic and fluorescent colours! Always follow the instructions on the packet before baking. Work on a board, and clean your work surface before you change colours.

Finish off salt-dough and papier mâché pieces by painting and varnishing them. Varnish also stops decorations from falling off, and protects fragile objects, such as leaves – after all, painting isn't the only way to decorate your jewellery.

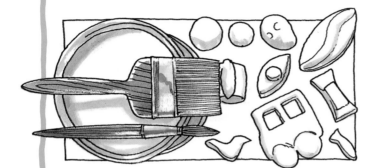
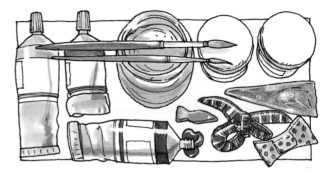

Paints and Brushes

Always let salt-dough jewellery cool, and papier mâché objects dry, before painting. Apply a coat of white emulsion first, so that you have a smooth, white surface to decorate. It will stop any newsprint showing through on your papier mâché pieces.

Acrylic paints are best if you want really dazzling results, but poster paints give bright colours too, and are much cheaper. Emulsion, acrylics and poster paints are all water-based, so all you'll need to clean your brushes is plenty of water.

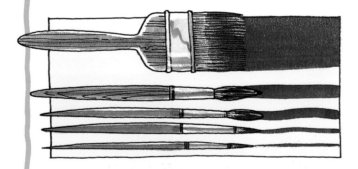
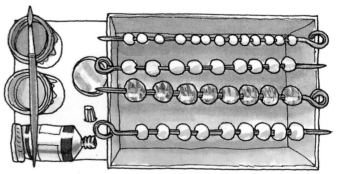

Keep a selection of brushes handy. A large, thick brush is best for emulsioning, but you'll need finer ones for painting details, especially on home-made beads.

When you have lots of beads to paint, thread them on a knitting needle. Rest the needle across an open shoe box, then paint. Leave the beads on the needle until they are all dry.

Using a cloth to rub gold paint on top of green will make your jewellery look like a valuable old antique!

Tricks with Paint

After emulsioning, apply a base colour. When this is dry, use a fine brush to paint a pattern on top.

Try smearing paint on to wood with your fingers. This gives an uneven and unusual stained effect.

Bits and Bobs

You can glue all sorts of daring decorations on to your jewellery. Use a strong epoxy glue, or white glue (PVA).

Gems, natural objects (such as seeds), and even string can all be used as unusual surface decorations. The only limit is your imagination!

Varnishing

Give all your painted jewellery a glossy coat of polyurethane varnish. It makes the paint really shine and stops it from chipping.

When varnishing, make sure there is enough air in the room. Varnish can be dangerous if you breathe in too much of it. Always keep the window wide open.

BRILLIANT BADGES

These badges will really brighten up a jacket or coat! We used coloured clay for the balloon and the musical badges, and added layers of clay to make raised patterns – this is called 'relief' decoration.

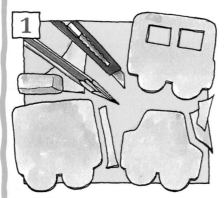

Salt-dough Badges

1 Draw and cut out simple shapes on card to use as templates for your badges.

2 Roll out a slab of salt dough to about 1 cm thick. Put the templates on the dough.

3 Now cut around the templates. You can cut out holes for windows too, if you want.

4 To mark the edges of the windows or wheels, dig into the dough with a fingernail or knife.

5 Bake the badges in the oven. Leave them to cool, then paint and varnish the fronts.

6 Stick a badge finding to the back, using a strong glue. Let the glue dry, then wear your badge!

To make this hot-air balloon, you'll need to roll very thin layers of coloured clay. Try not to smudge them!

Salt dough is just the thing for these chunky, colourful badges.

Musical Badges

1 Make templates for the guitar and keyboard. Place them on 0.5 cm-thick coloured clay and cut round them.

2 Cut out piano keys and the guitar trimmings, and press into place. Mark piano keys and guitar frets with a knife.

3 Bake the badges in the oven. When they are cool, use a strong glue to fix badge findings to the back.

11

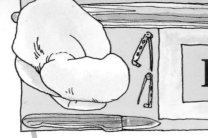

FLOWERS & BOWS

Salt-dough flowers and bows make pretty brooches. Bake all your pieces together, leave to cool and then paint and varnish. Finally, glue badge findings to the backs. Brooches make wonderful presents – if you can bear to give these ones away!

Bows

Roll out some salt dough to 0.5 cm thick. Then use a knife to cut a strip (1 x 15 cm), like a salt-dough ribbon.

small strip goes over the join

Loop the strip into a bow, as if it were a ribbon. Make joins wherever one layer overlaps another – just dab with water and press gently together. Use an extra scrap to cover the centre.

To make a bow-tie brooch, cut out a basic bow-tie shape, and a small rectangle (for the 'knot') from salt dough. Stick the knot on with a dab of water.

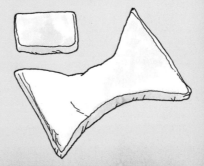

Flowers

Make a card template for the petals. Cut out about ten petals from salt dough.

Overlap the petals to make a circle. Dab with water to smooth the joins neatly.

Press a blob of dough in the centre of each flower to hide any messy joins.

For another kind of flower, cut the base with a pastry cutter. Stick four diamond-shaped petals on top.

You can also make flowers by sticking four smaller petals on top of four larger ones.

BANGLES & RINGS

Papier mâché is perfect for making fun, chunky jewellery. You can decorate rings with jewels made from scrunched-up tissue paper. Then use bright paints in different colours. Let each coat of paint dry before using a new colour. Always make sure your bangles and rings are big enough to slide on and off your wrist and fingers easily.

1 Cut two strips of thin card. Give one a wavy edge. Ask a friend to hold each strip around your wrist and tape the ends together for you.

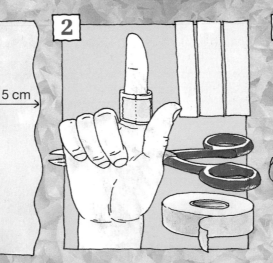

2 Cut narrower strips to make rings. Wrap them around your finger, so they slide off easily, then tape the ends together as before.

3 For a chunky bracelet, take six strips of newspaper and twist them together. Wrap this rope around your wrist and tape as before.

14

4 Cover the outside of all the pieces with three layers of papier mâché. If you take the strips over the edges, you'll get a smooth finish.

5 Scrunch up newspaper jewels for the rings. Tape them on and cover with one layer of papier mâché to give a smooth finish.

6 Paint a white emulsion base and then use bold acrylics. Rub gold paint on to the chunky bangle (see page 8). Finish off with a coat of varnish.

BEAD NECKLACES

Salt-dough beads look brilliant when you thread them with bought beads from craft shops. Try making round beads, then go for new shapes, such as the Egyptian eyes. Mix different types together – string big, homemade beads with tiny coloured glass ones.

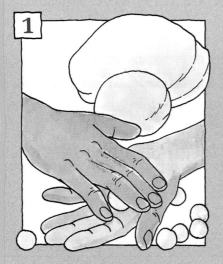

1 Pinch off a small piece of salt dough and roll it into a ball in your palm.

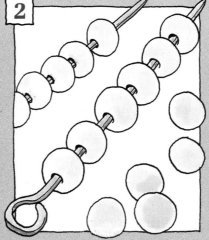

2 Push each bead on to a kebab skewer. Smooth each bead's surface.

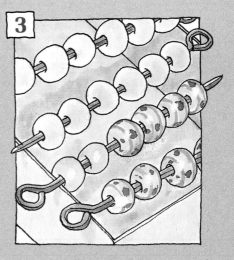

3 Bake the beads on their skewers. Paint and varnish when cool.

Threading Beads

Take a length of strong thread. Tape down one end with masking tape, (so your beads don't fall off), then thread on the beads with a needle. Peel off the tape and knot the ends of thread together. Feed the leftover thread neatly back through the beads.

Beads don't have to be round – these are shaped as Egyptian eyes! Push in a metal paper-clip before baking and thread them by the hooks.

For a lucky charm, tie red ribbon to a spare Egyptian eye bead. Pin the ribbon on with a safety pin.

BEACH-COMBING

The beach is a treasure-trove for jewellers! But shells can be tricky to drill, so it is usually easier to buy them with ready-drilled holes from a craft shop. Show off the shells by trying out these different ways of threading.

Drilling

If you do want to use shells that you've collected yourself, ask an adult to drill holes in them for you. They will need to use a drill with a fine bit. Always wash the shells first.

Threading Shells

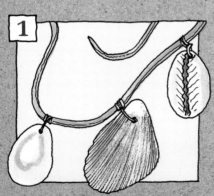

1

With some cotton, tie about three shells to the middle of a leather thong. Try using a coloured thong.

2

Thread a bead, then a shell, then go back through the first bead. Leave a space before threading the next two.

3

Knot a piece of string, thread on a shell, then knot again. Leave a space, then repeat with a bead. Keep swapping the beads and shells.

Jazz up your necklaces with textured threads – try using string, leather thongs or raffia.

Driftwood Pendant

Take a small piece of driftwood. Ask an adult to drill a hole in it.

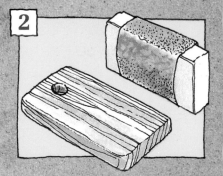

Smooth the edges of your driftwood. To make your own sander, wrap fine sandpaper around a block of wood.

Stain the wood with paint (see page 9) and glue on coiled spirals of string. Thread onto chunky cord or string.

Shells look great threaded with sea-blue glass beads.

EARRINGS

You can wear earrings whether your ears are pierced or not. Craft shops sell clip-on earring findings as well as ones for pierced ears. Glue clip-ons to the back of the finished earring.

Pierced Ears

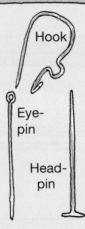

Hook

Eye-pin

Head-pin

Findings for pierced ears have two parts. The hook is the part that goes through your ear. It slips on to the pin. There are two different kinds of pin – head-pins and eye-pins.

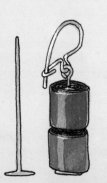

Head-pins are used for bead earrings. The head stops the beads falling off (see page 25). When the beads are in place, bend round the top of the pin with tweezers to make an eye for the hook.

Eye-pins are used for papier mâché or salt-dough earrings. They have an eye, but no head. Stick them into the earring so the eye pokes out at the top.

Salt Dough

Shape the salt dough – tiny fish and birds are easy and fun to do. Before baking, push in an eye-pin. After baking, painting and varnishing your earrings, slip the eye-pin over a hook.

Papier Mâché

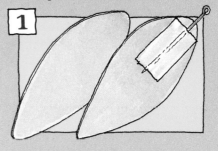

1

Start with a pair of shaped card bases. Tape an eye-pin to the base, so that the eye pokes out of the top.

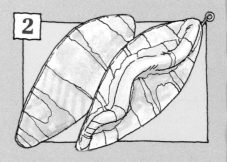

2

Cover with two layers of papier mâché. Make relief decorations with scrunched-up paper. When dry, emulsion, paint and varnish.

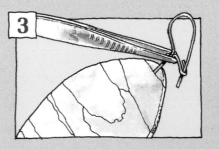

3

Slide the earring pin on to the hook by its eye. Squeeze the hook's wire with tweezers so the pin won't slip off.

For a really snazzy special effect, rub on sparkling gold paint before varnishing.

PIRATE ATTACK!

You could wear this necklace of ghoulish skulls and clattering bone beads with a pirate costume for a party. The tiger beads were made in the same way as the skulls.

To make your skulls and bones look really rotten, mix a drop of yellow paint in with the white.

Thread the orange tiger beads with bright green ready-made beads.

1

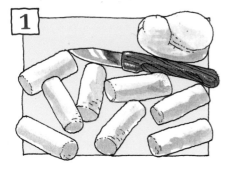

With your hands, roll some salt dough into a sausage shape about 30 cm long. Cut into eight pieces.

2

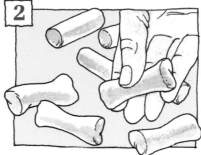

Shape each piece to look like a bone. It's best to pinch the dough in at the middle of the bone, and at both ends.

3

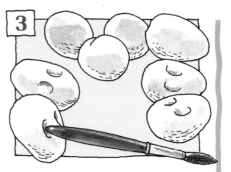

Roll eight balls of salt dough for the skulls. Squeeze in the cheeks. Use the end of a brush to make eye sockets.

4

Push all the beads on to kebab skewers and bake in the oven. When cool, give everything a coat of white paint.

5

For extra ghoul-appeal, use black paint to make your skulls' eyes, noses and mouths really stand out! Then varnish.

6

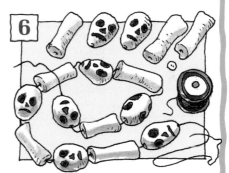

Thread the skulls and bones. Tie the ends of the thread to a button – it keeps the beads on as you thread them.

Bony Badge

Join two bones with a dab of water, to make the shape of a cross. Press a skull on top.

Smooth the back of the badge surface. Bake, paint and varnish, then glue on a badge finding.

SWEET TOOTH

Use coloured clay to make this delicious sweetie jewellery. Don't leave your beads lying around though – they look so realistic that someone might end up eating them!

1 Break off small lumps of clay. Roll into balls, then knock each one on your work surface to flatten the edges, until you get a cube shape.

2 Make stripey sweets by rolling out layers of different coloured clays. Press them on top of each other, then cut into squares.

3 Roll some clay into a long sausage with your fingers. Wrap a new colour around it and press gently. Smooth the join neatly.

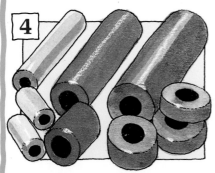

4 Cut the sausage shape into sweet-sized beads. Make more in the same way, but change the thickness and cut to different lengths.

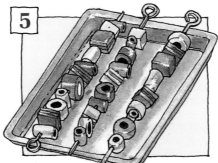

5 Push all your beads on to kebab skewers and bake them in the oven, on a baking tray. Follow the instructions on the packet carefully.

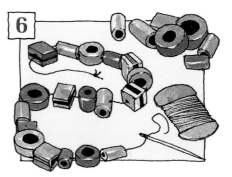

6 When the beads are all cool, thread them on fine elastic, then knot the ends. You can make a necklace and a matching bracelet.

Make smaller beads for earrings. Use earring findings with head-pins (see page 20).

PAPER JEWELLERY

Rolled paper beads may look delicate, but the wallpaper paste makes them surprisingly strong. Try using all sorts of coloured paper, in lots of different thicknesses, as well as newspapers and old glossy magazines.

For earring beads with a large hole, use an eye-pin (see page 20), and bend back the pin with tweezers.

1

Make card templates for your beads. Rectangles make simple tube beads. To make oval beads, use a triangle. For fat beads use long templates. For long beads, use wide templates.

2

Use the templates to cut out paper triangles and rectangles. To save time, fold the paper in a concertina and draw around the template. Then cut out lots of paper strips at once.

3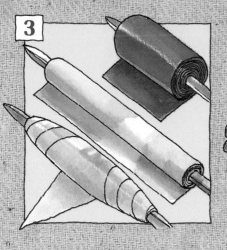

Coat both sides of each strip with paste, then roll around a skewer. Roll triangles from their base and rectangles from their short edge.

4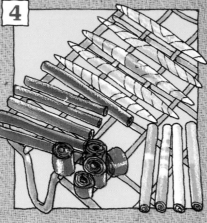

Slide the beads off the skewer and place on a wire rack to give the paste time to dry. There's no need to varnish the beads.

5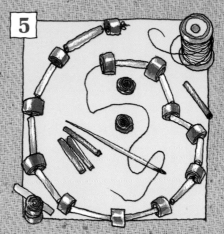

Thread the beads through their skewer holes, using strong, cotton thread. Finish off by tying the thread with a double knot.

You don't have to thread all the beads through their skewer holes. If you thread through the top, they look spiky. Try bunching a group together like this.

BACK TO NATURE

Natural objects make delicate, unusual necklaces. Collect seeds and leaves outdoors, or raid the kitchen for bay leaves and melon seeds – anything you can find! You'll need to wash melon seeds, place them on kitchen paper, and leave them to dry in a warm place for a few days. A coat of varnish will give the bay leaves extra strength and shine.

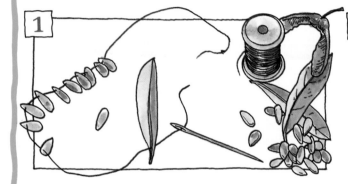

1 Thread a needle with cotton. Knot the end and then push the needle through about ten melon seeds. Thread a bay leaf next.

2 Swap between rows of melon seeds, and sycamore seeds or bay leaves. Tie a knot at the end to secure all the seeds and leaves.

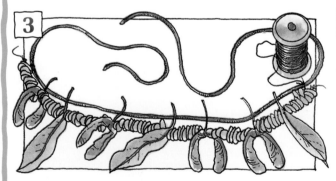

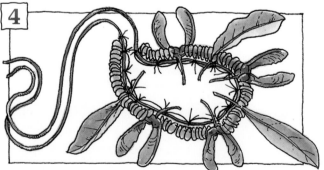

3 Take a length of cord about 80 cm long. Position the string of seeds in the middle. Now cut another piece of cotton and use it to tie one end of the row of seeds to the cord.

4 Use a double knot to attach the seeds to the cord, about every 2 cm along, until you reach the end. Knot the ends of the cord and your necklace is ready to wear!

Always ask an adult before you gather seeds. Some of them are poisonous.

FELT FRUITS

Squares of felt come in just about every colour of the rainbow. Felt is fabulous for making mouth-watering fruits like these.

Felt fruits look great pinned to your clothes, bag or a floppy sunhat. Or why not display them in a mini fruit basket?

1

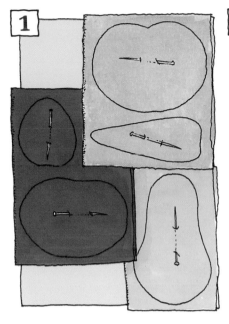

Draw templates for the tangerine, pear, carrot, tomato and strawberry on paper. Cut them out and pin to scraps of felt.

2

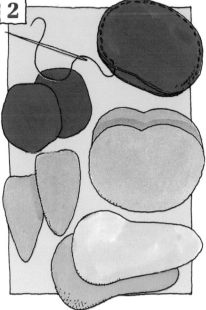

Cut around each template twice. Sew the two halves of each fruit together, leaving a small opening.

3

Stuff each fruit with cotton wool, then sew up the gap. Cut out felt leaves and sew to the top of each fruit.

4

To finish off, sew tiny coloured beads to the strawberries. Push a tiny safety pin through the back of each fruit.

A Bunch of Cherries

Stitch around a small circle of red felt, then tighten the thread to pull the felt into a ball. Stuff the opening with cotton wool, then finish sewing up the cherry.

Cut thin strips of felt for the stems. Fold in half and stitch down the edge. Sew one to each cherry and pin together in bunches. Add stems to the strawberries too.

SUPER SPECS

Make these swanky specs for when you feel like some larger-than-life dressing up! Design them in the wackiest shapes you can imagine. Use bold, vivid colours and paint on wild patterns. For the sunburst specs, build papier mâché sunrays across the eye holes, coming out of a bright Sun in the corner. Make sure you leave the slits wide enough for you to see through.

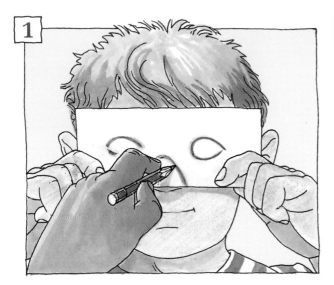

Measure across your face and cut a piece of thin card to this width. Hold it to your face and ask a friend to mark where your eyes and nose are.

Draw the outline of your glasses and cut them out carefully with a craft knife. Then measure and cut out a pair of arms for your glasses.

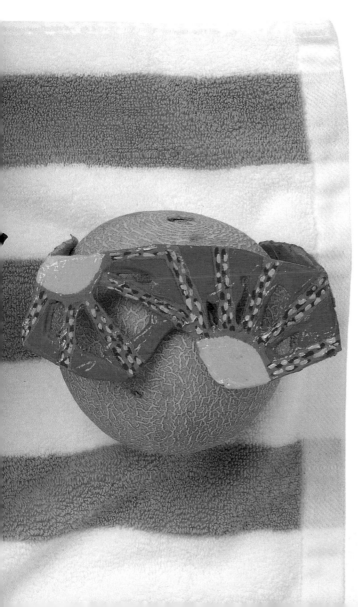

Make a hinge by taping the arms to the glasses with masking tape. Cover with about three layers of papier mâché. Keep the arm hinges moving as the layers dry, so you will be able to fold your finished glasses.

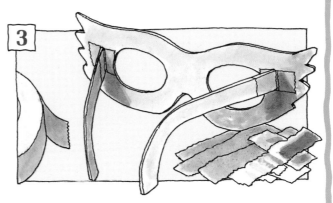

Coat the glasses with emulsion, then paint a dazzling pattern in bright acrylic paints. Finish off your super specs with a glossy layer of varnish.

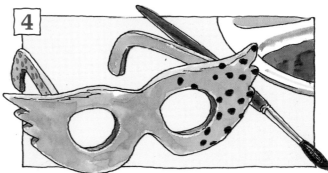

MEGA MEDALS

Ever felt you deserved a medal? Well, now you can sport one that's big enough for everyone to see! The giant fob-watch is papier mâché too.

Hang the medals on lengths of ribbon and use gold parcel string for the watch chain.

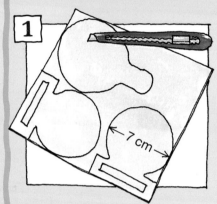

1 ← 7 cm →

Draw the shapes on to thin card and cut them out with a craft knife.

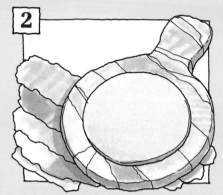

2 Cover the card bases with two layers of papier mâché. For a raised watch face, tape on a smaller circle and cover with one more layer.

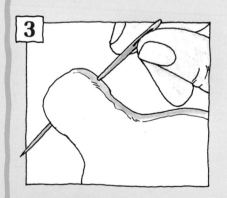

3

Emulsion, paint and varnish your pieces. Use a darning needle to pierce a hole through the top of the watch, for the chain. Re-open the hole after each coat of paint or varnish.

AZTEC JEWELLERY

The Aztec people lived in South America hundreds of years ago and their goldsmiths were famous for their dazzling jewellery. Make your own glittering Aztec necklace and a matching ceremonial headdress, encrusted with gems. Finish off with a flourish of bright, coloured feathers.

1
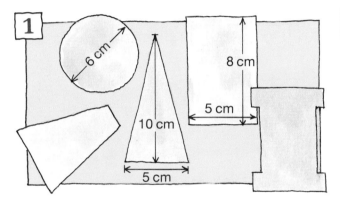

Cut out the necklace parts from card – you will need two rectangles, two triangles and a circle. Snip the tops of both triangles. Cut into the sides of one of the rectangles, as shown.

2
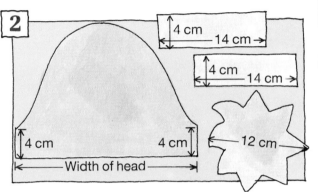

Measure the width of your head, then draw and cut out the headdress front, sides and star. Bend the headdress so it fits the shape of your head, and then tape on the sides.

3
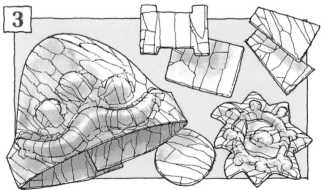

Cover all the shapes with three layers of papier mâché. Tape scrunched-up paper to the headdress and star for raised decoration (see page 21). Cover with a layer of papier mâché.

4

Glue spirals of string on to the necklace pieces for relief decoration. Pierce holes with a skewer, or darning needle, in the necklace pieces, headdress and star as shown.

5

Emulsion all your pieces. Then paint the star and necklace pieces a shiny, Aztec gold. Use jade-green for the headdress – the Aztecs loved jade.

6

When the headdress is dry, rub gold paint over the green with a cloth. Use a fine brush to paint extra details on all the pieces, then varnish.

7

Tie the necklace pieces together with short lengths of sparkling gold parcel string. Use gold raffia at the top to hang the necklace around your neck.

8

Glue brightly coloured feathers to the top of your headdress. Use garden wire to fix the star firmly on top, hiding the glue. Twist the wire at the back.

9

Glue bright felt streamers to the inside of the head-dress, so they flop over the top. To finish off, glue on gems, sequins and coils of string.

SHOWING OFF

Forget about boring old boxes! Why not show the pieces you have made on a crazy Mexican jewellery cactus! You can buy scrap wood for the base from a hardware store.

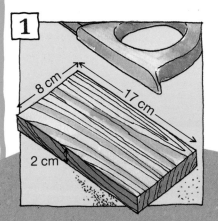

1

Ask an adult to saw a small block of wood (about 17 x 8 x 2 cm) to make a sturdy base.

2

Use masking tape to fix a cardboard tube, such as a toilet roll, to the wooden base.

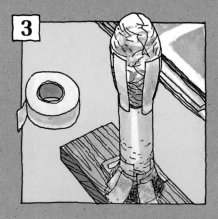

3

Crumple some paper, stuff it into the top of the tube, then tape it in place. This is for fixing your branches to.

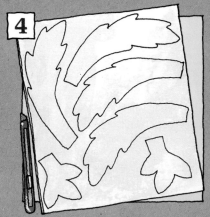

4

Cut out the branches from card with a craft knife. The two large ones have two halves, so cut out four of these.

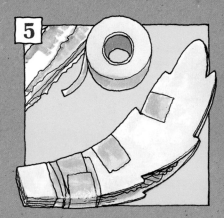

5

Stuff paper between the two halves of each large branch to pad it out. Hold the sides together with tape.

6 Tape all four branches to the cactus and cover everything with three layers of papier mâché.

7 Give the cactus a coat of emulsion then paint it bright green. Paint on yellow cactus spines, then varnish.

MORE IDEAS

By now you should have realised that almost anything can be turned into jewellery. Here are a few more ideas you might like to try . . .

Wind some raffia round and round a card bracelet. Sew embroidery thread in and out of the raffia, adding beads as you go.

Embroidery thread looks great plaited. Tie the ends to a hair grip, or knot them together to make a friendship bracelet. Add beads if you like.

For a choker, make a salt-dough heart with a hole in the middle. Use pink embroidery thread to sew the heart to a length of velvet ribbon. Glue on two Velcro™ squares for the fastening, or sew on press studs.

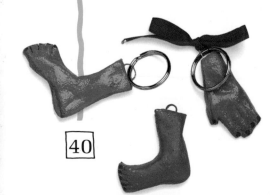

Use salt dough to make these jolly key-ring charms. Push in a paper-clip before baking. After painting, slide it on to a key-ring – you can buy them from shoe repair shops.